Efficiency Unleashed

Efficiency Unleashed

Introduction...

Let's face it. Staying productive on a consistent basis isn't easy - and this can be especially so when you run your own business from home.

Ok - so you might for example have quit your job to enjoy more freedom and be able to live life on your own terms. That's absolutely fantastic, however this brings a new and added problem...

When you're self employed and/or run your own business **everything is down to you...**

If you decide to waste away an entire day watching YouTube videos then nobody's going to come along and stop you or "tell you off." Getting what you need to get done is entirely your own responsibility - and if you want to be successful then it's important to be motivated and **know exactly how to stay productive on a consistent basis.**

That's exactly what this book's all about.

In the coming pages we're going to show you how to be more productive - right from creating a working environment that facilitates productivity through to everyday tips and tricks that you can use yourself.

Let's get into it...

Why is it so hard to stay productive?

As we have already mentioned, staying productive isn't easy - and most people are actually pretty bad at it.

So why is this the case?

For starters being productive requires a good deal of consistent discipline. It's all very well being productive for an entire morning - or even an entire day. But what about the next day? and the day after?

If you want to be truly productive then you're going to need to stay productive day in, day out. This means making the most of each and every working day and prioritising your tasks so that the most important things get done on time.

Organisation

One of the biggest reasons why many people struggle to stay productive is that they aren't organised enough. If you're constantly spending time finding files and locating the right information then it isn't a good situation for anybody and can really slow you down. This applies to both your computer and the workspace around you.

Not having a clear plan

People who are truly productive know what they need to do - and they know when they're doing it.

People who struggle with productivity on the other hand tend to go about tasks haphazardly. They often aren't clear on exactly what they need to do - and they definitely aren't good at prioritising the important stuff.

Distractions

Perhaps one of the biggest reasons many people struggle to stay productive is that they are surrounded by distractions.

Let's face it. Everyday life is full of distractions - whether they're online or offline - and eliminating these distractions (or at the very least reducing them) is absolutely critical to staying productive.

Distractions can be particularly problematic in the online world. I reckon we've all been in the situation where these distractions start to spiral out of control...

You see an interesting looking YouTube video and decide to watch it before you get stuck into your work. At the end of the video another one catches your eye and so you decide to watch that too. Inside that video something captures your imagination and so you decide to do a quick Google search to find out more. "Wow, I didn't know it was possible to do *that*" you say to yourself, before finding an entire resource on the subject. As you're browsing, an email notification window pops up telling you that you've received a message from someone you've been trying to get hold of for a while. You type out a reply and whilst you're in your inbox you notice an interesting looking email from your favourite marketer...

Can you see what's happening here?

Before you know it 3 hours have gone by and you haven't even started the original task you set out to do.

This is crazy - and yet it's an easy cycle to get into and one that millions of people find themselves struggling with every single day.

and distractions don't have to be online either. They can be in the form of the TV, radio and even your own friends and family. Each time you're kids come into your office and ask for something you're probably losing a LOT of time in terms of productivity. Sure, they might only come in and ask you a quick question before leaving again - but the problem is that it distracts you away from your thoughts. By the time you've re-focused and got back on track you've lost a lot more time than you probably think.

Ok - so in this book we're going to help you overcome some of these things and hopefully get you in a position where you're more productive than you've ever been before.

Are you excited about becoming more productive?

If you're not then you really **should** be. If you want to get more done each and every day then you've got to actually **WANT** to become productive. This isn't just going to happen without you making changes to the way you operate, ok?

What affects YOUR productivity?

The first thing we're going to have you do is to make a list of the things that personally affect your productivity. Not thing's that you *think* affect productivity in general but stuff that personally affects you.

Think long and hard about this, then open up your favourite note making software (or just grab a pen and paper) and make a list of all the things you think currently have a negative impact on your productivity.

Maybe you find email distracting? Maybe you're a sucker for Facebooking? Perhaps you have kids that constantly interrupt your working day? or perhaps you feel like you always lack focus?

As an example, your list might look something like this:

- My girlfriend regularly comes into my office and asks me questions.
- I spend too much time each day sorting through emails and have a very disorganised inbox.
- It takes me ages to find the files I'm looking for because I have documents scattered all over my desktop.
- I sometimes struggle to define my working time and my leisure time.
- I check Facebook too much.

etc

Once you have thought about all the things you feel are having a negative impact on your productivity then it becomes easier to improve the situation and take steps to tackle each one.

Once you've written down your list, take some time to think about each one and ask yourself what you could do to eliminate the distraction or problem.

Below each bullet point, write down an actionable step you could take.

For example:

- My girlfriend regularly comes into my office and asks me questions.
- **Action steps - Talk to my girlfriend and define my working hours. When I am working on project X and want no interruptions then I will talk to her about it beforehand. Keep my office door shut when I am working so as to create a defined workspace.**

- I spend too much time each day sorting through emails and have a very disorganised inbox.
- **Action step: I will not check my emails until I have completed at least the first two things on my daily to-do list. I will set aside 30 mins each afternoon to go through my inbox, delete emails I don't need and put the ones requiring action into a separate folder.**

- It takes me ages to find the files I'm looking for because I have documents scattered over multiple folders on my desktop.
- **Action step: Go to my computer desktop and put my files into folders. Delete all unnecessary files.**

- I sometimes struggle to define my working time and my leisure time.
- **Action step - I will stop checking my emails when sitting in front of the TV every night.**

- I check Facebook too much.
- **Action step: I will only allow myself to check Facebook between 12-1pm lunch time and after 6pm in the evening.**

These are obviously just examples - and you need to think about what solution you think would work best for you.

Set up your working environment

Being productive starts with creating a working environment that facilitates productivity...

What do I mean by this?

I'm talking about creating an office (or at least an assigned working space) which makes you feel comfortable and puts you in the right frame of mind to be productive. This is extremely important because you can have all the productivity knowledge in the world but if your working environment is uncomfortable and full of distractions then you're never going to be able to implement stuff and work to the best of your ability.

Decide where you're going to work from

The ideal scenario is that you have a separate home office from which to work, however the reality is that many people are tight on space and thus you might not be able to dedicate an entire room to your office. If this is the case then you should at least give yourself a dedicated corner or area of a room. Whilst it can be tempting to work from the kitchen table or the sofa this is also where you are most likely to be distracted. In addition doing so blurs the boundaries between work and home life much more than if you have a dedicated working space.

Your desk, keyboard and chair

Three important things to consider are your desk, keyboard and chair.

Let's start with the **desk.** This should be the right height for you so that you're not reaching up or down to your computer, and it should provide you with enough worktop space to be able to do your work in comfort. Think about your working tools such as your laptop, mouse, printer and notepad, and then choose a desk which has enough worktop space to be able to accommodate all of them whilst giving you room to spread things out.

Another important thing to consider is your **keyboard**. Whether you do most of your work on a laptop or a desktop it's important to choose one with a keyboard that's comfortable and fluent to type on. You don't want to be using a keyboard which is full of sticking keys and which makes your arms ache after ten minutes.

Whilst we are on this subject you might also want to think about the **mouse** you are using. If you're using a laptop/notebook with a trackpad at home then you might want to consider investing in a separate desktop-style mouse as many people find these easier and quicker to use.

Finally it is absolutely crucial that you have an office chair that you find comfortable to sit at for long periods of time. Most people who work from home are going to be spending perhaps around seven or eight hours a day sat at their desk so it's very important that you can do so in comfort and not have to suffer crippling backache. As well as choosing a chair that provides good body support it is also usually worthwhile to choose one that is height adjustable, thus allowing you to sit at your desk at the optimum height.

Lighting

People often forget this one but that doesn't mean it isn't important. You need to give yourself adequate lighting to be able to see and work in comfort. Don't just think about desk or room lighting either - the best working spaces provide lots of natural light and bring the outdoors in.

Get organized

If you want to be productive then it's SO important to get yourself organized, both in terms of your physical workspace and your computer workspace. Being organized will provide you with clarity and put you in the right frame of mind to work hard, not to mention make it easy to locate the things you need to do your work.

Have a place for everything and keep your desk worktop as clutter free as possible.

This one is really important. It can be hard to be truly productive if your desk is cluttered and piled high with documents, so try your best to keep things as organised as possible. Hide documents and files that you don't need away in drawers and aim to have a worktop that is free from clutter, with adequate space for a notepad. Don't just think about your desk either - make sure the entire office or working area is relatively tidy and free of junk.

Organise your desktop

One of the easiest ways of getting organized is to organize your computer desktop. Many people have files scattered all over it in a haphazard fashion - and not only does this make it time consuming to locate the files and folders you need it also looks untidy and sets you on the mindset that you are disorganized, which in turn can become an excuse for not being productive.

If your computer desktop is disorganised then go and tidy it up. Put all of your files into grouped folders and completely clear away all the ones you don't need.

Organize your email inbox

Most of us receive a LOT of emails each and every day, and for many people it is a constant battle to keep up to date with all the emails coming in from clients, marketers and other contacts.

Keeping your inbox tidy and organized is absolutely critical to achieving productivity in the modern world. If your inbox contains thousands of emails then it's easy to feel overwhelmed by them all, as well as meaning that you might miss the important emails that you really need to deal with.

If you find email a problem then consider using a tool such as SaneBox which will automatically filter out your unimportant emails so that you can concentrate on the ones you really need to read and/or deal with.

Each day it can be a good idea to go through your inbox and sort through the emails that have come in. You might, for example, set up two different folders such as "action required" and "read later" so that you can sort your emails into those two folders according to whether or not action is required. Emails that you don't want to read and don't require action can then simply be deleted so that they aren't cluttering up your inbox.

If you use Gmail, you can label everything accordingly and set up filters to automatically label emails with your client's name. You can even use filters to automatically move junk, so you don't have to waste time reading things that aren't valuable to you.

In addition if you have multiple email accounts then it can be a good idea to set up your accounts so that you can view all of your emails in one place. You can do this using a program such as Outlook, Apple Mail or even in Gmail.

Practical ways to increase your productivity

Ok, so by now you should be getting a pretty clear message that setting up a good workspace and being as organised as possible can have a massive impact on your productivity.

Now it's time to get into practical ways of increasing your productivity on a day to day basis. If you implement what we're going to talk about below then you'll go a long way towards getting more done in less time and being more productive on a consistent basis.

Making a great to-do list

To-do lists are probably one of the first things you think about when you approach the subject of productivity. They're something that millions of people use each and every day so that they know exactly what they need to get done, however aside from just writing down a list on a piece of paper there are a few things you can do to improve the effectiveness of them.

Make your list at the end of each day

The first thing to say is that you should consider making your to-do lists at the end of each day, rather than at the beginning. Most people will load up their computer in the morning, check their emails, check social media and *then* think about what they actually need to get done during the day ahead and write their list. This is often a bad idea because generally you will have wasted several hours in the morning before you've even made your to-do list and started on the first task. On the other hand if you make your to-do list at the end of each working day then you'll fire up your computer the following morning and be able to get stuck straight into the first task.

Prioritise each task

Another thing you can do is to put a number by each item on your to-do list according to its priority. So if you have five main items on your to-do list then you would number each one from 1 to 5, with 1 being the highest priority task and 5 being the lowest priority task. Again, this isn't really rocket science but you would be amazed by how many people fail to do it.

Don't put too many tasks on your list

Having a to-list that includes 30 items is just setting yourself up for failure. It's overwhelming - and it's probably unlikely that you'll be able to complete all of the tasks within a single day.

If you're struggling to reduce the size of your to-do lists then consider dropping your common tasks from the list altogether - for example "check email" is probably something that you will do anyway and might not need to be on your list at all.

Make each task specific

Having something like "update status on my Facebook fan page" is helpful to nobody. Instead, you should make each task highly specific - so it might be "Update the status on my Facebook fan page to thank people for coming to last night's seminar and link to the blog post on my website which discusses the evening's event."

Make each task achievable

It's important that each task on your daily to-do list is actually achievable in the day ahead - and you can do this by breaking down your bigger tasks into chunks or mini-tasks. If you were writing a book, for example, then it would be silly to have a to-do list task called "write my book." A much better idea would be to have it as "write 10 pages of my book" or "finish chapter 4."

Organizing your day

Do your most dreaded task first

This one is a biggie and can really set you up to be productive for the entire day. Most of us will find that there is a particular task on a given day that we're really not looking forward to, therefore by getting it out of the way first it will free your mind to do your other tasks later on, safe in the knowledge that the dreaded one is already done.

Again, this is a very simple tip but extremely powerful. We all have tasks that we dread and put off for as long as we can - but can you rest when it's NOT yet done? Nope, you keep thinking about it and it's generally on your mind. Nine times out of ten you then find that when you do finally get around to doing it it's not as bad as you even expected.

When do you work best?

When organising how you're going to spend your day it's important to think about when you work best. Some people are crazy productive first thing in the morning, whilst others prefer to work later on and maybe even in the evening. Generally speaking most people are productive at the beginning of their working time and then begin to flag as the day goes on.

Set your working hours - and then stick to them

One of the things people seem to struggle with when it comes to working from home is separating their home life from their working life. Thanks to smartphones and tablets it's very easy to start doing things like checking your emails in the evening whilst sitting in front of the TV - and before you know where you are you're never away from work.

At the same time it's easy for leisure activities such as browsing social media and watching YouTube videos to start creeping into the time when you should be working. Yep, it's those horrible distractions again.

Ideally you should set yourself a set working time - for example 9am to 5pm Monday to Thursday, with a lunch break between 1pm and 2pm. Let people around you know that this is your working time and that during these hours they should treat you as though you were actually at work in a corporate office - which means not disturbing you with family or social stuff.

Inside of your working hours you should try to be totally focused on work, however equally you should try not to do anything work related outside of the times you set. As touched on earlier, closing your office door is an added way of providing a separation between your working life and your leisure time.

Give yourself regular breaks

However you organize your working days it's important to give yourself regular breaks from tasks. Trying to focus for hours on end without a break is neither practical nor any good for your productivity levels!

Many people recommend working in short bursts - for example by working solidly for 60 minutes followed by a 10-minute break.

As an added point, taking a break means walking away from the computer and not just visiting Youtube for ten minutes. Removing yourself from your workstation gives your eyes a rest and helps remove your thoughts away from work for a little while.

Remember that you're not Superman!

When you work for yourself it's easy to overload yourself with work. Sometimes you're the director, the marketer, the admin person, the accountant and the technician all rolled into one - but never forget that you're not Superman. You just can't do everything yourself all of the time - and whilst it's ok to work extended long hours on some days in order to bring things up-to-date and keep clients happy you shouldn't be doing so on a consistent basis.

Each and every task you set yourself should be manageable and achievable. Setting yourself a goal of writing 100 pages a day for example is just not realistic and you're never going to achieve it. It's important to break tasks down into manageable chunks so that you keep yourself motivated over time.

If you regularly set yourself goals that are totally unrealistic then you're going to start getting unnecessarily down on yourself when you inevitably don't meet your goals.

Set yourself clear and realistic deadlines

In order to avoid continually putting tasks off you should always set yourself a clear deadline of when a particular thing needs to be finished by. Again your deadline should be realistic - you're not going to write 20 pages for example in the next half an hour!

Consider outsourcing

There are only so many hours in a day and no matter how good you believe you are it's impossible to do everything yourself – and not only is it impossible but it's also not a very good idea!

Consider outsourcing tasks in your business that you don't think are a very good use of your time. Let's imagine you spend 3 hours every day organizing your diary and booking client appointments. A good personal assistant will be able to do this for you and free up your time to concentrate on the really important stuff.

Go through every task you do and ask yourself if you really need to be doing it yourself or whether it could be cheaply outsourced to someone else. By outsourcing certain things in your business then you can free up your time like you wouldn't believe and for once be able to focus on important things that will grow your business.

As an added point nobody's good at everything – and if you're not very good at something (and/or you hate doing it) then the chances are that a.) it's going to take you longer to do and b.) you probably won't make a very good job of it. Many people out there will be able to do a better job at something than you could do yourself simply because that's where their particular skillset lies.

"Turn off" social media and email

Social media and email are two things that most people check every day (or every hour in some cases), however they are also two of the main things standing between you and true productivity.

Make it your goal to only check these things during set periods of the day. You might, for example, decide that you'll check your emails twice a day, at 11am in the morning and then again at 3pm, and that you will only check social media accounts such as Facebook and Twitter outside of your working hours.

If you have your laptop and smartphone set up to notify you of incoming messages or social media 'mentions' then consider turning off these features. You might, for example, have committed yourself to not checking social media during your working time, however how tempting is it going to be to check Facebook when your phone pings to notify you that you've just been tagged in a Facebook photo? It might only take a second to quickly look at the photo on Facebook but that can be extremely dangerous because it's taking your thoughts away from your work.

In addition, make sure chat features are set to "offline." Many people stay logged into social media accounts all day long and thus their friends will see that they are "online" and start a chat conversation with them. Remember that you're at work and that such things should ideally be limited to your down time, so make sure you're set to show as "offline" during your working time.

Productivity tools

There are lots of productivity tools out there that can help you with everything from note making and organising your day through to eliminating potential distractions.

Here are a few different tools to consider…

StayFocusd

This handy tool can help you limit the amount of time you spend on time-wasting websites.

Evernote

A very popular and powerful note making tool.

Todo.ly

A potentially useful tool for creating online to-do lists.

Cool Clock

This handy browser extension can help you with a whole manner of different things – including a stopwatch to time your tasks, hourly desktop time notifications and integration with your calendar.

Conclusion

Staying truly productive on a consistent basis requires effort – and it's definitely not an easy thing to do. If you're prepared to take action and change the way you do things however then an increase in productivity can truly transform your life.

One of the keys to productivity is setting yourself up with the right working environment. You could know all the productivity tips in the world but if your working time is uncomfortable and/or full of distractions then you're never going to get much done.

Equally being organized is SO important if you want to be truly productive. Disorganization not only means it will take you longer to find the things you need to do your work but it can also leave you feeling overwhelmed and/or confused, which is never good for productivity. If you can stay reasonably organized AND you know how to plan out your day and prioritize the important stuff then you're definitely going along the right road.

I hope you found this report useful and that it's provided you with some good advice and strategies on how to increase your productivity. Now it's really up to you…

So, what are you waiting for? Get out there and get your work done!